Cornwall E.L.S

CORNWALL EDUCATION LIBRARY SERVICE	
915.95	11-Aug-2017
£12.99	PETERS

MALAYSIA
WORLD ADVENTURES
BY STEFFI CAVELL-CLARKE

BookLife

©2017
Book Life
King's Lynn
Norfolk PE30 4LS

ISBN: 978-1-78637-193-5

All rights reserved
Printed in Malaysia

Written by:
Steffi Cavell-Clarke

Edited by:
Charlie Ogden

Designed by:
Gareth Liddington

A catalogue record for this book is available from the British Library.

MALAYSIA
WORLD ADVENTURES

CONTENTS

Page 4	Where Is Malaysia?
Page 6	Weather and Landscape
Page 8	Clothing
Page 10	Religion
Page 12	Food
Page 14	At School
Page 16	At Home
Page 18	Families
Page 20	Sport
Page 22	Fun Facts
Page 24	Glossary and Index

Words in **bold** can be found in the glossary on page 24.

WHERE IS MALAYSIA?

Malaysia is a country in Southeast Asia. Malaysia is made up of two large pieces of land and lots of small **islands** in the South China Sea.

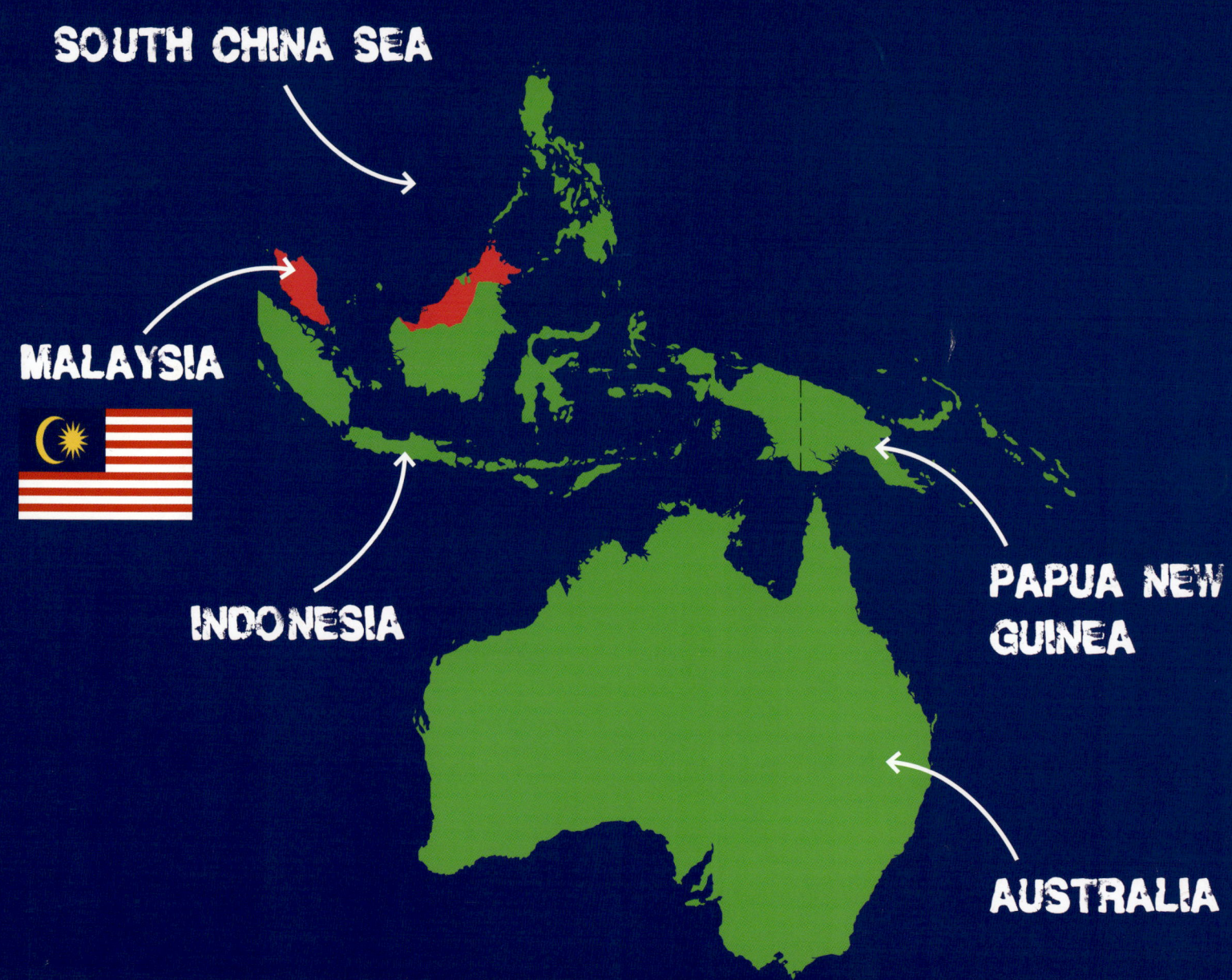

The capital city of Malaysia is called Kuala Lumpur. It is home to over eight million people, but millions more visit every year to see and experience the city.

PETRONAS TWIN TOWERS

CHINATOWN

WEATHER AND LANDSCAPE

Malaysia is located near to the **equator**. This means that it has a **tropical climate** and the weather is usually hot and wet all year round.

There are many different landscapes in Malaysia. There are tall mountains, tropical rainforests and long beaches.

Mount Kinabalu is the tallest mountain in Malaysia.

Lots of animals live in Malaysia's tropical rainforests.

CLOTHING

Malaysia is home to many different **cultures**. Some people wear the **traditional** clothes of their culture and others wear casual clothing.

The Malaysian traditional dress for men is a long tunic worn over trousers with a sampin wrapped around the hips. Men also often wear a songkok.

RELIGION

The religion in Malaysia with the most followers is Islam.

Many different **religions** are practised in Malaysia, such as Buddhism, Christianity, Hinduism and traditional Chinese religions.

Many different festivals are celebrated in Malaysia every year. One of the biggest festivals is Eid al-Fitr, which celebrates the end of **Ramadan**.

FOOD

Malaysia's **national** dish is nasi lemak, a rice dish cooked in coconut milk. Rice is a common dish in Malaysia and is often eaten with meat or vegetables.

Eating outside is a big part of Malaysian culture. Every night, streets in Malaysian cities are lined with restaurants and stalls selling street food.

Street food in Kuala Lumpur, Malaysia.

AT SCHOOL

School children in Malaysia have to wear school uniforms. They are expected to be well-behaved and study hard.

Children are taught to read and write Malay, which is the most spoken language in Malaysia. They are also taught other subjects such as English, maths, science and history.

AT HOME

There are lots of different types of home in Malaysia. Many people live in apartments in tall tower blocks. Other people live in houses.

TOWER BLOCKS

HOUSES

Traditional Malaysian houses were made out of bamboo and wood. They were built on stilts to protect the people living there from floods and wild animals.

FAMILIES

In Malaysia, parents usually live together with their children in a family home. Family is very important in Malaysia.

Elderly people are supported and respected by members of their family.

Religious families often pray together at their place of **worship**. There are Islamic places of worship, known as mosques, and Buddhist temples in most towns and cities.

MOSQUE

BUDDHIST TEMPLE

SPORT

A popular sport in Malaysia is sepak takraw. This game involves two teams of three players, a net and a ball.

Each team must hit the ball over the net to the other team, but they can only use their feet, knees, chest and head. No hands are allowed!

Children practice sepak takraw after school.

FUN FACTS

The national animal of Malaysia is the Malayan tiger.

Malaysia is home to the largest flower in the world, called the Rafflesia arnoldii.

Malaysia is one of the few places where orangutans live in the wild. 'Orangutan' is a Malay word that means 'person of the forest'.

The tallest statue in Malaysia is the Lord Murugan Statue, which is 42.7 metres high.

Malaysia is home to one of the oldest rainforests in the world. Taman Negara is more than 130 million years old.

The Petronas Towers were the tallest buildings in the world from 1998 to 2004.

GLOSSARY

cultures	the traditions, ideas and ways of life of different groups of people
equator	the imaginary line around the Earth that is an equal distance from the North and South Poles
islands	areas of land surrounded by water
national	relating to, characteristic of or common to a nation
Ramadan	a month of fasting for Muslims
religions	the belief in and worship of a god or gods
traditional	related to very old behaviours or beliefs
tropical climate	warm and wet weather
worship	a religious act such as praying

INDEX

animals 7, 17, 22
cities 5, 13, 19
clothes 8
festivals 11
food 12–13
houses 16–17
Kuala Lumpur 5, 13
Malay 15, 22
mountains 7
rainforests 7, 23
religion 10–11, 19
school 14, 21

Photocredits: Abbreviations: l-left, r-right, b-bottom, t-top, c-centre, m-middle. All images are courtesy of Shutterstock.com.
Front Cover – ANUCHA PONGPATIMETH, bg – Aleksey Klints. 2 – Leonid Andronov. 5l – nelzajamal. 5r – Migel. 6 – Fhaizal Mazlan. 7t – Yusnizam Yusof. 7b – Sainam51. 8 – Suriya99. 9 – wong yu liang. 10 – TY Lim. 11 – Mansoreh. 12 – Ti Santi. 13 – hkhtt hj. 14 – Sharif Putra Sharif Ubong. 15 – Lano Lan. 16l – alex7370. 16r – Mawardi Bahar. 17 – Alex Edmonds. 18 – Aizuddin Saad. 19t – Aisyaqilumaranas. 19m – Nokuro. 19b – Leonid Andronov. 20 – sippakorn. 21 – Lano Lan. 22m – Nokuro. 22 – Muhammad Izzat 22br – ashadhodhomei. 23r – Araya Gerabun. 23tl – Cneo Osman. 23bl – Martin Pfeiffer. Images are courtesy of Shutterstock.com. With thanks to Getty Images, Thinkstock Photo and iStockphoto.